50 Decadent Chocolate Desserts

By: Kelly Johnson

Table of Contents

- Chocolate Lava Cake
- Chocolate Mousse
- Chocolate Fondue
- Chocolate Truffles
- Chocolate Tiramisu
- Chocolate Cheesecake
- Chocolate Eclairs
- Chocolate Soufflé
- Chocolate Fudge Brownies
- Chocolate Chip Cookies
- Chocolate Panna Cotta
- Chocolate Dipped Strawberries
- Chocolate Almond Cake
- Chocolate Pudding
- Chocolate Meringue Pie
- Flourless Chocolate Cake
- Chocolate Ganache Tart
- Chocolate-Covered Pretzels
- Chocolate Croissants
- Hot Chocolate Cupcakes
- Chocolate Ice Cream
- Chocolate Crepes
- Chocolate Bread Pudding
- Chocolate-Dipped Marshmallows
- Chocolate Hazelnut Spread
- Chocolate-Coconut Macaroons
- Chocolate-Covered Cherries
- Chocolate Pavlova
- Chocolate-Coffee Cake
- Chocolate Peanut Butter Pie
- Chocolate Scones
- Chocolate Banana Bread
- Chocolate Ricotta Pie
- Chocolate Cannoli
- Chocolate Mint Brownies

- Chocolate Tart with Raspberry Sauce
- Chocolate Fudge
- Chocolate Waffles
- Chocolate Caramel Cake
- Chocolate Eclairs with Vanilla Cream
- Chocolate Biscotti
- Chocolate Ice Cream Sandwiches
- Chocolate Pistachio Cake
- Chocolate Orange Pudding
- Chocolate Pecan Pie
- Chocolate Chip Banana Muffins
- Chocolate Zucchini Cake
- Chocolate Cherry Clafoutis
- Chocolate Chip Blondies
- Chocolate Churros

Chocolate Lava Cake

Ingredients:

- 1/2 cup unsalted butter
- 6 oz semi-sweet chocolate, chopped
- 1 cup powdered sugar
- 2 large eggs
- 2 large egg yolks
- 1 tsp vanilla extract
- 1/4 cup all-purpose flour
- Pinch of salt
- Butter and cocoa powder for greasing the ramekins

Instructions:

1. **Prep the ramekins**:
   Preheat the oven to 425°F (220°C). Grease four ramekins with butter, then dust with cocoa powder to prevent sticking.
2. **Melt chocolate**:
   In a heatproof bowl, melt the butter and chocolate together over a double boiler or microwave. Stir until smooth.
3. **Mix batter**:
   Whisk in the powdered sugar, then add eggs, egg yolks, and vanilla extract. Stir in the flour and a pinch of salt until just combined.
4. **Fill ramekins**:
   Pour the batter into the prepared ramekins, filling each about 3/4 full.
5. **Bake**:
   Bake for 12-14 minutes or until the edges are set but the center is soft. Let them cool for 1 minute, then carefully invert onto plates.
6. **Serve**:
   Serve warm with vanilla ice cream or whipped cream.

Chocolate Mousse

Ingredients:

- 8 oz semi-sweet chocolate, chopped
- 1 cup heavy cream
- 1/4 cup powdered sugar
- 1 tsp vanilla extract
- 2 large egg whites
- Pinch of salt

Instructions:

1. **Melt chocolate:**
   Melt the chocolate in a heatproof bowl over simmering water or microwave in intervals, stirring until smooth. Let cool slightly.
2. **Whip cream:**
   In a chilled bowl, whip the heavy cream with powdered sugar and vanilla extract until soft peaks form. Set aside.
3. **Whisk egg whites:**
   In a separate bowl, beat the egg whites with a pinch of salt until stiff peaks form.
4. **Combine:**
   Gently fold the whipped cream into the melted chocolate, then fold in the egg whites until smooth.
5. **Chill:**
   Spoon the mousse into serving glasses and chill for at least 2 hours before serving.

Chocolate Fondue

Ingredients:

- 8 oz semi-sweet or milk chocolate, chopped
- 1/2 cup heavy cream
- 2 tbsp sugar (optional)
- 1 tsp vanilla extract
- Fruit, marshmallows, and cubes of cake for dipping

Instructions:

1. **Melt chocolate:**
   In a heatproof bowl, combine chocolate and cream. Place over a simmering pot of water (double boiler) or microwave in intervals, stirring until smooth.
2. **Add flavor:**
   Stir in sugar and vanilla extract, then mix until fully combined.
3. **Serve:**
   Transfer the melted chocolate to a fondue pot, and serve with fruits, marshmallows, and cake cubes for dipping.

Chocolate Truffles

Ingredients:

- 8 oz semi-sweet or dark chocolate, chopped
- 1/2 cup heavy cream
- 2 tbsp unsalted butter
- Cocoa powder or melted chocolate for coating

Instructions:

1. **Melt chocolate:**
   Heat the cream in a saucepan until it begins to simmer. Pour it over the chopped chocolate and let sit for 1-2 minutes, then stir until smooth.
2. **Add butter:**
   Stir in the butter until fully combined.
3. **Chill the mixture:**
   Let the mixture cool to room temperature, then refrigerate for 1-2 hours until firm.
4. **Form truffles:**
   Using a spoon, scoop small amounts of the chocolate mixture and roll them into balls. Coat them in cocoa powder or melted chocolate.
5. **Serve:**
   Store truffles in the fridge until ready to serve.

Chocolate Tiramisu

Ingredients:

- 8 oz mascarpone cheese
- 1/2 cup heavy cream
- 1/2 cup powdered sugar
- 1 tsp vanilla extract
- 6 oz dark chocolate, melted
- 24 ladyfingers
- 1 cup strong coffee or espresso, cooled
- Cocoa powder for dusting

Instructions:

1. **Make filling**:
   Whisk together mascarpone, heavy cream, powdered sugar, and vanilla extract in a bowl. Add melted chocolate and whisk until smooth.
2. **Prepare coffee**:
   Dip ladyfingers in the cooled coffee for a few seconds and layer them at the bottom of a dish.
3. **Layer**:
   Spread a layer of the chocolate mascarpone mixture over the ladyfingers. Repeat layers of dipped ladyfingers and mascarpone mixture.
4. **Chill**:
   Refrigerate for at least 4 hours or overnight for best flavor.
5. **Serve**:
   Dust the top with cocoa powder before serving.

Chocolate Cheesecake

Ingredients:

- 2 cups graham cracker crumbs
- 1/4 cup sugar
- 1/2 cup unsalted butter, melted
- 3 (8 oz) packages cream cheese, softened
- 1 cup sour cream
- 1 cup sugar
- 1 tsp vanilla extract
- 1/2 cup cocoa powder
- 4 oz semi-sweet chocolate, melted
- 3 large eggs

Instructions:

1. **Prepare crust**:
   Preheat the oven to 325°F (160°C). In a bowl, combine graham cracker crumbs, sugar, and melted butter. Press into the bottom of a springform pan and bake for 10 minutes.
2. **Make filling**:
   In a large bowl, beat cream cheese until smooth. Add sour cream, sugar, vanilla, and cocoa powder, and beat until combined. Add melted chocolate and eggs, beating until smooth.
3. **Bake**:
   Pour the filling over the crust and bake for 55-60 minutes, or until the edges are set and the center slightly jiggles.
4. **Cool**:
   Let the cheesecake cool to room temperature, then refrigerate for at least 4 hours before serving.

Chocolate Eclairs

Ingredients:

- **For the dough:**
    - 1/2 cup water
    - 1/2 cup unsalted butter
    - 1 cup all-purpose flour
    - 4 large eggs
    - 1 tbsp sugar
    - Pinch of salt
- **For the filling:**
    - 1 1/2 cups heavy cream
    - 1 tbsp powdered sugar
    - 1 tsp vanilla extract
- **For the glaze:**
    - 4 oz semi-sweet chocolate, chopped
    - 2 tbsp heavy cream

Instructions:

1. **Make the dough:**
   Preheat the oven to 400°F (200°C). In a saucepan, bring water and butter to a boil. Stir in the flour, sugar, and salt. Cook for 2 minutes. Remove from heat, let cool slightly, then beat in eggs one at a time until smooth.
2. **Pipe the dough:**
   Pipe the dough onto a lined baking sheet into 3-inch long logs. Bake for 25-30 minutes, until puffed and golden.
3. **Make the filling:**
   Whip the heavy cream, powdered sugar, and vanilla extract until soft peaks form. Transfer to a piping bag.
4. **Make the glaze:**
   Heat the chocolate and cream in a saucepan over low heat until melted and smooth.
5. **Assemble:**
   Slice the eclairs, pipe in the cream, and dip the tops in the chocolate glaze. Let cool before serving.

Chocolate Soufflé

Ingredients:

- 4 oz semi-sweet chocolate, chopped
- 1 tbsp unsalted butter
- 1/4 cup heavy cream
- 2 large egg yolks
- 3 large egg whites
- 1/4 cup sugar
- 1 tsp vanilla extract
- Powdered sugar for dusting

Instructions:

1. **Prepare ramekins**:
   Preheat the oven to 375°F (190°C). Butter and sugar the sides of four ramekins.
2. **Melt chocolate**:
   Melt chocolate, butter, and heavy cream together in a bowl over simmering water. Remove from heat and whisk in egg yolks and vanilla.
3. **Whisk egg whites**:
   In a separate bowl, whisk the egg whites with sugar until stiff peaks form.
4. **Combine**:
   Gently fold the egg whites into the chocolate mixture until combined.
5. **Bake**:
   Spoon the mixture into the ramekins and bake for 12-15 minutes, until puffed and set.
6. **Serve**:
   Dust with powdered sugar and serve immediately.

Chocolate Fudge Brownies

Ingredients:

- 1 cup unsalted butter
- 8 oz semi-sweet chocolate, chopped
- 1 1/2 cups sugar
- 1 tsp vanilla extract
- 3 large eggs
- 1 cup all-purpose flour
- 1/2 cup unsweetened cocoa powder
- 1/2 tsp salt
- 1/2 tsp baking powder

Instructions:

1. **Prep the pan**:
   Preheat the oven to 350°F (175°C). Grease and line a 9x9-inch baking pan with parchment paper.
2. **Melt chocolate and butter**:
   In a saucepan, melt the butter and chopped chocolate together over low heat, stirring until smooth. Let cool slightly.
3. **Mix the batter**:
   Whisk sugar and vanilla extract into the chocolate mixture. Add eggs one at a time, beating well after each addition. Stir in flour, cocoa powder, salt, and baking powder.
4. **Bake**:
   Pour the batter into the prepared pan and bake for 25-30 minutes, or until a toothpick comes out with just a few moist crumbs.
5. **Cool**:
   Let the brownies cool before cutting into squares and serving.

Chocolate Chip Cookies

Ingredients:

- 1 cup unsalted butter, softened
- 3/4 cup granulated sugar
- 3/4 cup packed brown sugar
- 1 tsp vanilla extract
- 2 large eggs
- 2 1/4 cups all-purpose flour
- 1 tsp baking soda
- 1/2 tsp salt
- 2 cups semi-sweet chocolate chips

Instructions:

1. **Prep the oven and pan**:
   Preheat the oven to 350°F (175°C). Line baking sheets with parchment paper.
2. **Cream butter and sugars**:
   In a large bowl, beat together butter, granulated sugar, brown sugar, and vanilla extract until creamy. Add eggs, one at a time, mixing well.
3. **Mix dry ingredients**:
   In a separate bowl, combine flour, baking soda, and salt. Gradually add to the wet ingredients, mixing until just combined.
4. **Add chocolate chips**:
   Stir in chocolate chips.
5. **Shape and bake**:
   Drop spoonfuls of dough onto the prepared baking sheets. Bake for 10-12 minutes or until golden brown.
6. **Cool**:
   Allow cookies to cool on a wire rack before serving.

Chocolate Panna Cotta

Ingredients:

- 1 cup heavy cream
- 1/2 cup whole milk
- 1/2 cup sugar
- 4 oz semi-sweet chocolate, chopped
- 1 tsp vanilla extract
- 1 packet unflavored gelatin (about 2 tsp)
- 2 tbsp cold water

Instructions:

1. **Prepare gelatin:**
   In a small bowl, sprinkle gelatin over cold water and let it bloom for 5 minutes.
2. **Heat cream and milk:**
   In a saucepan, combine heavy cream, milk, and sugar. Heat over medium heat, stirring until the sugar dissolves.
3. **Add chocolate:**
   Remove from heat and stir in chopped chocolate until smooth.
4. **Combine gelatin:**
   Stir the bloomed gelatin into the warm cream mixture until fully dissolved.
5. **Chill:**
   Pour the mixture into serving glasses or molds and refrigerate for at least 4 hours or overnight until set.
6. **Serve:**
   Serve chilled, optionally with whipped cream or fruit.

Chocolate Dipped Strawberries

Ingredients:

- 1 lb fresh strawberries, washed and dried
- 8 oz semi-sweet or milk chocolate, chopped
- 2 tbsp vegetable oil (optional)

Instructions:

1. **Prep strawberries**:
   Ensure the strawberries are completely dry. Set aside.
2. **Melt chocolate**:
   In a heatproof bowl, melt the chocolate with vegetable oil over a double boiler or microwave in short intervals, stirring until smooth.
3. **Dip strawberries**:
   Hold each strawberry by the stem and dip it into the melted chocolate, covering about two-thirds of the berry.
4. **Cool**:
   Place dipped strawberries on a parchment-lined tray and let the chocolate harden at room temperature or in the refrigerator.
5. **Serve**:
   Serve as a sweet treat or gift.

Chocolate Almond Cake

Ingredients:

- 1 1/2 cups almond flour
- 1/2 cup cocoa powder
- 1 tsp baking soda
- 1/2 tsp salt
- 1/2 cup unsalted butter, softened
- 1 cup sugar
- 3 large eggs
- 1 tsp vanilla extract
- 1/2 cup milk
- 1/2 cup semi-sweet chocolate chips (optional)

Instructions:

1. **Prep the oven:**
   Preheat the oven to 350°F (175°C). Grease and line a 9-inch round cake pan.
2. **Mix dry ingredients:**
   In a bowl, whisk together almond flour, cocoa powder, baking soda, and salt.
3. **Cream butter and sugar:**
   In a separate bowl, cream together butter and sugar until light and fluffy. Add eggs, one at a time, and vanilla extract.
4. **Combine:**
   Gradually add dry ingredients and milk to the butter mixture, stirring until smooth. Fold in chocolate chips if using.
5. **Bake:**
   Pour the batter into the prepared pan and bake for 25-30 minutes, or until a toothpick comes out clean.
6. **Cool:**
   Allow the cake to cool before serving.

Chocolate Pudding

Ingredients:

- 1/2 cup granulated sugar
- 1/3 cup unsweetened cocoa powder
- 1/4 cup cornstarch
- 1/8 tsp salt
- 2 3/4 cups whole milk
- 3 large egg yolks
- 2 tbsp unsalted butter
- 1 tsp vanilla extract

Instructions:

1. **Mix dry ingredients:**
   In a saucepan, whisk together sugar, cocoa powder, cornstarch, and salt.
2. **Add milk:**
   Gradually add milk while whisking to avoid lumps. Heat the mixture over medium heat, stirring constantly.
3. **Temper eggs:**
   In a separate bowl, whisk the egg yolks. Gradually add a small amount of the hot milk mixture to temper the eggs, then whisk the egg mixture back into the saucepan.
4. **Cook the pudding:**
   Continue to cook and stir until the pudding thickens and starts to boil. Remove from heat.
5. **Finish and chill:**
   Stir in butter and vanilla extract. Pour into serving dishes and refrigerate for at least 2 hours before serving.

Chocolate Meringue Pie

Ingredients:

- **For the crust:**
    - 1 1/2 cups graham cracker crumbs
    - 1/4 cup sugar
    - 1/3 cup unsalted butter, melted
- **For the filling:**
    - 1 cup sugar
    - 1/3 cup unsweetened cocoa powder
    - 3 tbsp cornstarch
    - 1/8 tsp salt
    - 2 3/4 cups milk
    - 4 large egg yolks
    - 2 tbsp unsalted butter
    - 1 tsp vanilla extract
- **For the meringue:**
    - 4 large egg whites
    - 1/2 tsp cream of tartar
    - 1/2 cup sugar

Instructions:

1. **Make the crust:**
   Preheat the oven to 350°F (175°C). Mix graham cracker crumbs, sugar, and melted butter. Press into a pie dish and bake for 10 minutes. Let cool.
2. **Make the filling:**
   In a saucepan, whisk together sugar, cocoa powder, cornstarch, and salt. Gradually add milk, then cook over medium heat, whisking constantly, until thickened. Stir in egg yolks and cook for another 2 minutes. Remove from heat and stir in butter and vanilla.
3. **Make the meringue:**
   Beat egg whites and cream of tartar until soft peaks form. Gradually add sugar and continue to beat until stiff peaks form.
4. **Assemble and bake:**
   Pour the chocolate filling into the cooled crust. Spoon the meringue on top and bake at 350°F (175°C) for 10-15 minutes until the meringue is golden.
5. **Cool:**
   Allow to cool before serving.

Flourless Chocolate Cake

Ingredients:

- 1 cup unsalted butter
- 8 oz semi-sweet chocolate, chopped
- 1 cup granulated sugar
- 1/4 tsp salt
- 1 tsp vanilla extract
- 4 large eggs
- 1/2 cup unsweetened cocoa powder

Instructions:

1. **Prep the oven**:
   Preheat the oven to 375°F (190°C). Grease and flour an 8-inch round cake pan.
2. **Melt chocolate and butter**:
   In a saucepan, melt butter and chopped chocolate over low heat until smooth.
3. **Mix**:
   Stir sugar, salt, and vanilla extract into the chocolate mixture. Add eggs, one at a time, and mix well. Stir in cocoa powder.
4. **Bake**:
   Pour the batter into the pan and bake for 20-25 minutes. The cake will be soft in the center but firm around the edges.
5. **Cool**:
   Allow the cake to cool before serving. Top with powdered sugar or whipped cream.

Chocolate Ganache Tart

Ingredients:

- **For the crust:**
    - 1 1/2 cups graham cracker crumbs
    - 1/4 cup sugar
    - 1/3 cup unsalted butter, melted
- **For the ganache:**
    - 8 oz semi-sweet chocolate, chopped
    - 1 cup heavy cream
    - 2 tbsp unsalted butter

Instructions:

1. **Make the crust:**
   Preheat the oven to 350°F (175°C). Combine graham cracker crumbs, sugar, and melted butter. Press into a tart pan and bake for 8-10 minutes. Let cool.
2. **Make the ganache:**
   Heat cream in a saucepan until simmering. Pour over chopped chocolate and let sit for a minute. Stir until smooth, then mix in butter.
3. **Assemble the tart:**
   Pour ganache into the cooled crust. Refrigerate for 2-3 hours until set.
4. **Serve:**
   Garnish with fresh berries or whipped cream before serving.

Chocolate-Covered Pretzels

Ingredients:

- 2 cups mini pretzels
- 8 oz semi-sweet chocolate, chopped
- 2 tbsp vegetable oil
- 1/4 cup white chocolate (optional, for drizzling)

Instructions:

1. **Prepare pretzels**:
   Lay mini pretzels on a baking sheet lined with parchment paper.
2. **Melt chocolate**:
   In a heatproof bowl, melt semi-sweet chocolate and vegetable oil over a double boiler or microwave in short bursts, stirring until smooth.
3. **Dip pretzels**:
   Dip each pretzel into the melted chocolate, allowing any excess to drip off. Place on the baking sheet.
4. **Optional drizzle**:
   If using, melt white chocolate and drizzle over the dipped pretzels for decoration.
5. **Cool**:
   Let the chocolate set at room temperature or in the refrigerator for faster results.

Chocolate Croissants

Ingredients:

- 1 sheet puff pastry (store-bought)
- 1/2 cup semi-sweet chocolate chips
- 1 egg (for egg wash)

Instructions:

1. **Prep the oven:**
   Preheat the oven to 400°F (200°C) and line a baking sheet with parchment paper.
2. **Prepare the pastry:**
   Roll out the puff pastry sheet on a floured surface. Cut into triangles (about 6-8 per sheet).
3. **Fill and roll:**
   Place a small handful of chocolate chips at the wide end of each triangle. Roll up the pastry from the wide end to the point.
4. **Egg wash:**
   Beat the egg and brush over the top of each croissant for a golden finish.
5. **Bake:**
   Bake for 12-15 minutes, or until golden brown and puffed. Let cool slightly before serving.

Hot Chocolate Cupcakes

Ingredients:

- 1 1/2 cups all-purpose flour
- 1/2 cup cocoa powder
- 1 tsp baking powder
- 1/2 tsp baking soda
- 1/2 tsp salt
- 1/2 cup unsalted butter, softened
- 1 cup sugar
- 2 large eggs
- 1 tsp vanilla extract
- 1/2 cup milk
- 1/2 cup hot chocolate (prepared)
- 1 cup mini marshmallows (optional)

Instructions:

1. **Prep the oven:**
   Preheat the oven to 350°F (175°C) and line a muffin tin with cupcake liners.
2. **Mix dry ingredients:**
   In a bowl, whisk together flour, cocoa powder, baking powder, baking soda, and salt.
3. **Cream butter and sugar:**
   Beat butter and sugar together until light and fluffy. Add eggs one at a time, mixing well after each addition.
4. **Add wet ingredients:**
   Stir in the vanilla extract and milk. Gradually add the dry ingredients, alternating with hot chocolate, mixing until smooth.
5. **Bake:**
   Divide the batter evenly among the cupcake liners. Bake for 18-22 minutes, or until a toothpick comes out clean.
6. **Add marshmallows:**
   Optionally, top with mini marshmallows during the last 5 minutes of baking to toast them slightly.

Chocolate Ice Cream

Ingredients:

- 2 cups heavy cream
- 1 cup whole milk
- 1 cup granulated sugar
- 1/2 cup unsweetened cocoa powder
- 1 tsp vanilla extract
- 4 large egg yolks

Instructions:

1. **Mix the base**:
   In a saucepan, heat milk, cream, sugar, and cocoa powder over medium heat until the sugar is dissolved.
2. **Prepare egg yolks**:
   In a separate bowl, whisk egg yolks. Gradually add a small amount of the hot milk mixture to temper the eggs, then whisk the egg mixture back into the saucepan.
3. **Thicken**:
   Cook the mixture over low heat, stirring constantly, until thickened and coats the back of a spoon.
4. **Chill**:
   Remove from heat and stir in vanilla extract. Let the mixture cool to room temperature, then refrigerate for at least 4 hours.
5. **Churn**:
   Once chilled, churn the mixture in an ice cream maker according to the manufacturer's instructions.
6. **Freeze**:
   Transfer to a container and freeze for at least 4 hours before serving.

Chocolate Crepes

Ingredients:

- 1 cup all-purpose flour
- 2 tbsp cocoa powder
- 1 1/2 cups milk
- 2 large eggs
- 1/4 cup melted butter
- 2 tbsp sugar
- 1 tsp vanilla extract
- 1/4 tsp salt

Instructions:

1. **Make batter**:
   In a bowl, whisk together flour, cocoa powder, sugar, and salt. Add eggs, milk, melted butter, and vanilla extract. Mix until smooth.
2. **Cook crepes**:
   Heat a non-stick skillet over medium heat and lightly grease. Pour about 1/4 cup of batter into the pan, swirling to coat the bottom evenly.
3. **Flip**:
   Cook for about 1-2 minutes per side, until set. Flip and cook for another 30 seconds.
4. **Serve**:
   Stack crepes and fill with your favorite chocolate spread, fruits, or whipped cream.

Chocolate Bread Pudding

Ingredients:

- 4 cups day-old bread, cubed
- 2 cups whole milk
- 1 cup heavy cream
- 1 cup sugar
- 3 large eggs
- 1 tsp vanilla extract
- 1/2 cup semi-sweet chocolate chips

Instructions:

1. **Prep the oven:**
   Preheat the oven to 350°F (175°C) and grease a 9x9-inch baking dish.
2. **Prepare the custard:**
   In a bowl, whisk together eggs, sugar, milk, heavy cream, and vanilla extract.
3. **Combine bread and custard:**
   Add the cubed bread to the baking dish. Pour the custard mixture over the bread, pressing down gently to ensure the bread absorbs the custard.
4. **Add chocolate chips:**
   Sprinkle chocolate chips over the top.
5. **Bake:**
   Bake for 40-45 minutes, or until golden and set in the middle. Let cool slightly before serving.

Chocolate-Dipped Marshmallows

Ingredients:

- 1 bag marshmallows
- 8 oz semi-sweet chocolate, chopped
- Sprinkles, crushed nuts, or other toppings (optional)

Instructions:

1. **Melt chocolate**:
   Melt chocolate over a double boiler or microwave in short bursts, stirring until smooth.
2. **Dip marshmallows**:
   Hold each marshmallow by the stick and dip it into the melted chocolate, coating halfway.
3. **Decorate**:
   Optionally, dip the chocolate-covered marshmallow into sprinkles or crushed nuts.
4. **Cool**:
   Place on a parchment-lined tray and refrigerate until the chocolate sets.

Chocolate Hazelnut Spread

Ingredients:

- 1 cup hazelnuts, roasted and peeled
- 1/4 cup powdered sugar
- 1/4 cup cocoa powder
- 1/2 tsp vanilla extract
- 1/4 tsp salt
- 1/4 cup vegetable oil

Instructions:

1. **Process hazelnuts:**
   In a food processor, pulse hazelnuts until they form a smooth paste.
2. **Add other ingredients:**
   Add powdered sugar, cocoa powder, vanilla extract, and salt, and continue processing.
3. **Add oil:**
   Gradually add vegetable oil and blend until smooth and spreadable.
4. **Store:**
   Transfer to a jar and store in the refrigerator. Enjoy on toast, crepes, or desserts.

Chocolate-Coconut Macaroons

Ingredients:

- 2 cups sweetened shredded coconut
- 1/2 cup semisweet chocolate chips, melted
- 2 large egg whites
- 1/4 cup granulated sugar
- 1/2 tsp vanilla extract

Instructions:

1. **Preheat the oven:**
   Preheat the oven to 350°F (175°C) and line a baking sheet with parchment paper.
2. **Mix coconut and egg whites:**
   In a large bowl, mix shredded coconut, egg whites, sugar, and vanilla extract until well combined.
3. **Form macaroons:**
   Use a spoon or your hands to form small mounds of the coconut mixture on the baking sheet.
4. **Bake:**
   Bake for 15-20 minutes, or until the tops are golden brown.
5. **Dip in chocolate:**
   Once cooled, dip the bottoms of the macaroons into melted chocolate and let set.

Chocolate-Covered Cherries

Ingredients:

- 1 jar maraschino cherries, drained
- 8 oz semi-sweet chocolate, chopped
- 2 tbsp vegetable oil
- 1/4 tsp vanilla extract (optional)

Instructions:

1. **Prepare cherries:**
   Pat the maraschino cherries dry with paper towels to remove excess moisture. Set aside.
2. **Melt chocolate:**
   In a heatproof bowl, melt the semi-sweet chocolate and vegetable oil over a double boiler or in the microwave in 30-second intervals, stirring until smooth. Add vanilla extract if desired.
3. **Dip cherries:**
   Hold each cherry by the stem and dip it into the melted chocolate, coating it completely. Allow excess chocolate to drip off.
4. **Cool:**
   Place the chocolate-covered cherries on a parchment-lined tray and refrigerate for 1-2 hours, or until the chocolate sets.

Chocolate Pavlova

Ingredients:

- 4 large egg whites
- 1 cup granulated sugar
- 2 tbsp cocoa powder
- 1/2 tsp vanilla extract
- 1/2 tsp white vinegar
- 1/2 cup heavy cream
- 2 tbsp powdered sugar
- 1/2 tsp vanilla extract
- 1/2 cup chocolate shavings (for garnish)

Instructions:

1. **Preheat the oven**:
   Preheat the oven to 300°F (150°C) and line a baking sheet with parchment paper.
2. **Make meringue**:
   In a clean, dry bowl, beat egg whites until soft peaks form. Gradually add sugar, one tablespoon at a time, beating until stiff peaks form. Fold in cocoa powder, vanilla extract, and white vinegar.
3. **Form Pavlova**:
   Spoon the meringue mixture onto the prepared baking sheet, shaping it into a circular nest with a slight indentation in the center.
4. **Bake**:
   Bake for 1 hour, then turn off the oven and allow the meringue to cool completely inside the oven.
5. **Whip cream**:
   Whip the heavy cream with powdered sugar and vanilla extract until soft peaks form.
6. **Assemble**:
   Once the meringue is cooled, top with whipped cream and garnish with chocolate shavings.

Chocolate-Coffee Cake

Ingredients:

- 1 1/2 cups all-purpose flour
- 1/2 cup unsweetened cocoa powder
- 1 1/2 tsp baking powder
- 1/2 tsp baking soda
- 1/4 tsp salt
- 1/2 cup unsalted butter, softened
- 1 cup sugar
- 2 large eggs
- 1 tsp vanilla extract
- 1/2 cup sour cream
- 1/2 cup brewed coffee (cooled)
- 1/4 cup chocolate chips (optional)
- 1/4 cup chopped walnuts (optional)

Instructions:

1. **Preheat the oven**:
   Preheat the oven to 350°F (175°C) and grease a 9-inch round cake pan.
2. **Mix dry ingredients**:
   In a medium bowl, whisk together flour, cocoa powder, baking powder, baking soda, and salt.
3. **Cream butter and sugar**:
   In a large bowl, beat the softened butter and sugar until light and fluffy. Add eggs one at a time, followed by vanilla extract.
4. **Alternate dry ingredients and liquids**:
   Gradually add the dry ingredients to the butter mixture, alternating with sour cream and coffee. Mix until smooth.
5. **Bake**:
   Pour the batter into the prepared pan and sprinkle with chocolate chips and walnuts (optional). Bake for 30-35 minutes or until a toothpick inserted comes out clean. Let cool before serving.

Chocolate Peanut Butter Pie

Ingredients:

- 1 pre-made graham cracker crust
- 1 cup creamy peanut butter
- 8 oz cream cheese, softened
- 1 cup powdered sugar
- 1 cup heavy cream
- 1 tsp vanilla extract
- 8 oz semi-sweet chocolate, chopped
- 1 tbsp butter

Instructions:

1. **Prepare the filling**:
   Beat together peanut butter, cream cheese, and powdered sugar until smooth. In a separate bowl, whip heavy cream with vanilla extract until soft peaks form. Gently fold the whipped cream into the peanut butter mixture.
2. **Prepare the chocolate layer**:
   Melt the chocolate and butter in a heatproof bowl over a double boiler or in the microwave. Stir until smooth and let it cool slightly.
3. **Assemble the pie**:
   Spread the peanut butter filling into the graham cracker crust. Drizzle the melted chocolate over the top, swirling it to create a marbled effect.
4. **Chill**:
   Refrigerate the pie for at least 4 hours or overnight before serving.

Chocolate Scones

Ingredients:

- 2 cups all-purpose flour
- 1/4 cup unsweetened cocoa powder
- 1/4 cup sugar
- 2 1/2 tsp baking powder
- 1/4 tsp baking soda
- 1/4 tsp salt
- 1/2 cup cold unsalted butter, cubed
- 1/2 cup semi-sweet chocolate chips
- 1/2 cup buttermilk
- 1 tsp vanilla extract
- 1 egg, beaten (for egg wash)

Instructions:

1. **Preheat the oven**:
   Preheat the oven to 400°F (200°C) and line a baking sheet with parchment paper.
2. **Mix dry ingredients**:
   In a large bowl, whisk together flour, cocoa powder, sugar, baking powder, baking soda, and salt.
3. **Cut in butter**:
   Add cubed butter to the flour mixture and cut it in using a pastry cutter or your fingers until the mixture resembles coarse crumbs.
4. **Add chocolate chips**:
   Stir in the chocolate chips.
5. **Add wet ingredients**:
   In a separate bowl, whisk together buttermilk and vanilla extract. Add to the dry ingredients and stir until just combined.
6. **Form scones**:
   Turn the dough out onto a floured surface and gently knead. Pat the dough into a round shape and cut into 8 wedges. Place on the prepared baking sheet.
7. **Egg wash and bake**:
   Brush the tops of the scones with the beaten egg and bake for 15-18 minutes, or until golden brown.

Chocolate Banana Bread

Ingredients:

- 1 1/2 cups all-purpose flour
- 1/2 cup unsweetened cocoa powder
- 1 tsp baking soda
- 1/4 tsp salt
- 1/2 cup unsalted butter, softened
- 1 cup sugar
- 2 ripe bananas, mashed
- 2 large eggs
- 1 tsp vanilla extract
- 1/2 cup buttermilk
- 1/2 cup semi-sweet chocolate chips

Instructions:

1. **Preheat the oven:**
   Preheat the oven to 350°F (175°C) and grease a 9x5-inch loaf pan.
2. **Mix dry ingredients:**
   In a medium bowl, whisk together flour, cocoa powder, baking soda, and salt.
3. **Cream butter and sugar:**
   In a large bowl, beat together butter and sugar until light and fluffy. Add mashed bananas, eggs, and vanilla extract and mix until smooth.
4. **Combine wet and dry ingredients:**
   Gradually add the dry ingredients to the banana mixture, alternating with buttermilk. Stir in chocolate chips.
5. **Bake:**
   Pour the batter into the prepared loaf pan and bake for 60-70 minutes, or until a toothpick inserted comes out clean. Let cool before slicing.

Chocolate Ricotta Pie

Ingredients:

- 1 pre-made pie crust
- 1 1/2 cups ricotta cheese
- 1/2 cup sugar
- 1/2 cup unsweetened cocoa powder
- 2 large eggs
- 1 tsp vanilla extract
- 1/4 cup heavy cream
- 1/4 cup semi-sweet chocolate chips

Instructions:

1. **Preheat the oven**:
   Preheat the oven to 350°F (175°C) and place the pie crust in a pie dish.
2. **Prepare the filling**:
   In a bowl, beat together ricotta cheese, sugar, cocoa powder, eggs, vanilla extract, and heavy cream until smooth.
3. **Add chocolate chips**:
   Stir in chocolate chips.
4. **Bake**:
   Pour the filling into the prepared crust and bake for 45-50 minutes, or until the filling is set. Let cool before serving.

Chocolate Cannoli

Ingredients:

- 12 cannoli shells (store-bought or homemade)
- 2 cups ricotta cheese, drained
- 1/2 cup powdered sugar
- 1/2 cup mini chocolate chips
- 1 tsp vanilla extract
- 1/4 cup cocoa powder (for dusting)
- 1/4 cup chopped pistachios (optional, for garnish)

Instructions:

1. **Prepare filling**:
   In a bowl, mix ricotta cheese, powdered sugar, mini chocolate chips, and vanilla extract until smooth.
2. **Stuff cannoli shells**:
   Using a pastry bag or spoon, carefully fill each cannoli shell with the ricotta mixture.
3. **Dust and garnish**:
   Dust the filled cannoli with cocoa powder and garnish with chopped pistachios, if desired.

Chocolate Mint Brownies

Ingredients:

- 1/2 cup unsalted butter, melted
- 1 cup granulated sugar
- 2 large eggs
- 1 tsp vanilla extract
- 1/4 tsp peppermint extract
- 1/2 cup all-purpose flour
- 1/4 cup unsweetened cocoa powder
- 1/4 tsp salt
- 1/2 cup semi-sweet chocolate chips
- 1/4 cup heavy cream
- 1/4 tsp peppermint extract (for frosting)
- 1 cup powdered sugar

Instructions:

1. **Preheat the oven:**
   Preheat the oven to 350°F (175°C) and grease a 9x9-inch baking pan.
2. **Make brownie batter:**
   In a large bowl, combine melted butter, sugar, eggs, vanilla extract, and peppermint extract. Stir in flour, cocoa powder, and salt until well combined. Fold in chocolate chips.
3. **Bake:**
   Pour the batter into the prepared pan and bake for 20-25 minutes, or until a toothpick inserted comes out clean.
4. **Prepare frosting:**
   In a small bowl, mix heavy cream, peppermint extract, and powdered sugar until smooth. Spread over the cooled brownies.

Chocolate Tart with Raspberry Sauce

Ingredients:

- **For the crust:**
    - 1 1/2 cups all-purpose flour
    - 1/4 cup cocoa powder
    - 1/2 cup unsalted butter, cold and cubed
    - 1/4 cup powdered sugar
    - 1 large egg yolk
    - 2-3 tbsp cold water
- **For the filling:**
    - 8 oz semi-sweet chocolate, chopped
    - 1 cup heavy cream
    - 1/4 cup sugar
    - 1 tsp vanilla extract
- **For the raspberry sauce:**
    - 1 cup fresh raspberries
    - 1/4 cup sugar
    - 2 tbsp water

Instructions:

1. **Prepare the crust:**
   Preheat the oven to 350°F (175°C). In a food processor, combine flour, cocoa powder, butter, and powdered sugar. Pulse until the mixture resembles coarse crumbs. Add egg yolk and water, and pulse until the dough comes together. Press the dough into the bottom of a tart pan and refrigerate for 30 minutes. Bake the crust for 15-20 minutes, then cool.
2. **Make the filling:**
   Heat heavy cream in a saucepan over medium heat until it begins to simmer. Remove from heat and add chopped chocolate. Stir until smooth, then add sugar and vanilla extract. Pour the filling into the cooled crust and refrigerate for at least 3 hours to set.
3. **Make the raspberry sauce:**
   In a saucepan, combine raspberries, sugar, and water. Simmer over medium heat for 5-7 minutes until the raspberries break down. Strain the sauce through a fine mesh sieve to remove seeds.
4. **Assemble:**
   Once the tart has set, drizzle with raspberry sauce before serving.

Chocolate Fudge

Ingredients:

- 2 cups semi-sweet chocolate chips
- 1/2 cup sweetened condensed milk
- 1/4 cup unsalted butter
- 1/2 tsp vanilla extract
- 1/4 tsp salt

Instructions:

1. **Prepare the fudge:**
   Line an 8x8-inch baking pan with parchment paper. In a saucepan, melt butter and sweetened condensed milk over low heat. Stir in chocolate chips and continue stirring until completely melted. Add vanilla extract and salt.
2. **Set the fudge:**
   Pour the mixture into the prepared pan and spread evenly. Refrigerate for at least 2 hours, or until firm. Cut into squares before serving.

Chocolate Waffles

Ingredients:

- 2 cups all-purpose flour
- 1/4 cup cocoa powder
- 1/2 cup sugar
- 1 tbsp baking powder
- 1/4 tsp salt
- 1 3/4 cups milk
- 2 large eggs
- 1/2 cup unsalted butter, melted
- 1 tsp vanilla extract
- 1/2 cup chocolate chips

Instructions:

1. **Prepare the batter**:
   In a large bowl, whisk together flour, cocoa powder, sugar, baking powder, and salt. In a separate bowl, mix milk, eggs, melted butter, and vanilla extract. Pour the wet ingredients into the dry ingredients and stir until smooth. Fold in chocolate chips.
2. **Cook the waffles**:
   Preheat your waffle iron. Lightly grease it and pour the batter onto the iron, cooking according to the manufacturer's instructions, usually for about 3-5 minutes, or until golden brown. Serve with whipped cream or syrup.

Chocolate Caramel Cake

Ingredients:

- **For the cake:**
    - 1 3/4 cups all-purpose flour
    - 1 cup sugar
    - 1/4 cup unsweetened cocoa powder
    - 1 tsp baking powder
    - 1/2 tsp baking soda
    - 1/2 tsp salt
    - 1 cup buttermilk
    - 1/2 cup unsalted butter, melted
    - 2 large eggs
    - 1 tsp vanilla extract
- **For the caramel sauce:**
    - 1 cup brown sugar
    - 1/2 cup unsalted butter
    - 1/4 cup heavy cream
    - 1 tsp vanilla extract

Instructions:

1. **Prepare the cake:**
   Preheat the oven to 350°F (175°C) and grease two 9-inch round cake pans. In a large bowl, mix flour, sugar, cocoa powder, baking powder, baking soda, and salt. Add buttermilk, melted butter, eggs, and vanilla extract, and mix until smooth. Pour the batter evenly into the prepared pans.
2. **Bake the cake:**
   Bake for 25-30 minutes or until a toothpick inserted comes out clean. Let the cakes cool in the pans for 10 minutes, then transfer to wire racks to cool completely.
3. **Make the caramel sauce:**
   In a saucepan, combine brown sugar, butter, and heavy cream. Bring to a simmer over medium heat, stirring constantly. Let it simmer for 3-5 minutes until it thickens, then remove from heat and stir in vanilla extract.
4. **Assemble the cake:**
   Once the cakes are completely cooled, drizzle with caramel sauce and serve.

Chocolate Eclairs with Vanilla Cream

Ingredients:

- **For the choux pastry**:
    - 1 cup water
    - 1/2 cup unsalted butter
    - 1 cup all-purpose flour
    - 1/4 tsp salt
    - 4 large eggs
- **For the vanilla cream**:
    - 2 cups heavy cream
    - 1/2 cup powdered sugar
    - 1 tsp vanilla extract
- **For the chocolate glaze**:
    - 4 oz semi-sweet chocolate, chopped
    - 1/4 cup heavy cream

Instructions:

1. **Make the choux pastry**:
   Preheat the oven to 400°F (200°C) and line a baking sheet with parchment paper. In a saucepan, combine water and butter, bringing it to a boil. Add flour and salt, stirring until the mixture pulls away from the sides of the pan. Remove from heat and let cool for 5 minutes. Add eggs one at a time, beating well after each addition.
2. **Shape and bake**:
   Spoon the dough into a piping bag and pipe 3-inch long strips onto the baking sheet. Bake for 20-25 minutes, or until puffed and golden brown. Let cool.
3. **Make the vanilla cream**:
   In a mixing bowl, whip heavy cream, powdered sugar, and vanilla extract until stiff peaks form.
4. **Assemble the eclairs**:
   Once the eclairs are cooled, slice them open and fill with vanilla cream. Drizzle with chocolate glaze.
5. **Make the chocolate glaze**:
   In a heatproof bowl, melt the chocolate and heavy cream together until smooth. Drizzle over the filled eclairs before serving.

Chocolate Biscotti

Ingredients:

- 2 cups all-purpose flour
- 1 cup sugar
- 1/4 cup unsweetened cocoa powder
- 1 tsp baking powder
- 1/2 tsp salt
- 2 large eggs
- 1 tsp vanilla extract
- 1/2 cup chocolate chips

Instructions:

1. **Prepare the dough**:
   Preheat the oven to 350°F (175°C) and line a baking sheet with parchment paper. In a large bowl, mix flour, sugar, cocoa powder, baking powder, and salt. Add eggs and vanilla extract, mixing until combined. Stir in chocolate chips.
2. **Shape the dough**:
   Divide the dough in half and shape each half into a log on the prepared baking sheet. Bake for 25-30 minutes or until firm. Let the logs cool for 10 minutes, then slice them diagonally into 1/2-inch pieces.
3. **Bake the biscotti**:
   Arrange the slices back on the baking sheet and bake for an additional 10-15 minutes, flipping halfway through. Cool completely before serving.

Chocolate Ice Cream Sandwiches

Ingredients:

- **For the cookies**:
    - 1 1/2 cups all-purpose flour
    - 1/2 cup unsweetened cocoa powder
    - 1/2 tsp baking soda
    - 1/4 tsp salt
    - 1/2 cup unsalted butter, softened
    - 1 cup sugar
    - 1 large egg
    - 1 tsp vanilla extract
- **For the filling**:
    - 2 cups chocolate ice cream, softened

Instructions:

1. **Make the cookies**:
   Preheat the oven to 350°F (175°C) and line a baking sheet with parchment paper. In a medium bowl, whisk together flour, cocoa powder, baking soda, and salt. In a separate bowl, cream together butter and sugar. Add the egg and vanilla extract and mix until smooth. Gradually add the dry ingredients, mixing until just combined.
2. **Shape and bake**:
   Scoop spoonfuls of dough onto the baking sheet and flatten slightly. Bake for 8-10 minutes or until set. Cool completely.
3. **Assemble the sandwiches**:
   Once the cookies have cooled, spread a generous amount of softened chocolate ice cream on the bottom of one cookie and top with another to form a sandwich. Freeze for at least 1 hour before serving.

Chocolate Pistachio Cake

Ingredients:

- 1 1/2 cups all-purpose flour
- 1/2 cup cocoa powder
- 1 tsp baking powder
- 1/2 tsp salt
- 1/2 cup unsalted butter, softened
- 1 cup sugar
- 2 large eggs
- 1 tsp vanilla extract
- 1/2 cup milk
- 1/2 cup chopped pistachios

Instructions:

1. **Prepare the cake:**
   Preheat the oven to 350°F (175°C) and grease a 9-inch cake pan. In a bowl, combine flour, cocoa powder, baking powder, and salt. In a separate bowl, cream together butter and sugar. Add eggs one at a time, followed by vanilla extract. Gradually add the dry ingredients, alternating with the milk, and mix until smooth. Fold in chopped pistachios.
2. **Bake the cake:**
   Pour the batter into the prepared cake pan and bake for 25-30 minutes, or until a toothpick inserted comes out clean. Let the cake cool before serving.

Chocolate Orange Pudding

Ingredients:

- 2 cups milk
- 1/2 cup sugar
- 1/4 cup cocoa powder
- 1/4 cup cornstarch
- 1/4 tsp salt
- 2 large egg yolks
- 2 tbsp unsalted butter
- 1 tsp vanilla extract
- Zest of 1 orange
- 1/4 cup fresh orange juice

Instructions:

1. **Make the pudding:**
   In a saucepan, combine milk, sugar, cocoa powder, cornstarch, and salt. Cook over medium heat, whisking constantly until the mixture thickens. Once thickened, remove from heat.
2. **Temper the eggs:**
   In a small bowl, whisk the egg yolks. Gradually add a bit of the hot pudding mixture to the yolks, whisking constantly. Slowly return the egg mixture to the saucepan and cook for another 2-3 minutes, stirring constantly.
3. **Finish the pudding:**
   Remove the pudding from heat and stir in the butter, vanilla extract, orange zest, and orange juice. Pour the pudding into individual bowls and refrigerate for at least 2 hours before serving.

Chocolate Pecan Pie

Ingredients:

- 1 pie crust (store-bought or homemade)
- 1 cup dark corn syrup
- 1/2 cup brown sugar, packed
- 4 large eggs
- 1/4 cup unsalted butter, melted
- 1 tsp vanilla extract
- 1/4 tsp salt
- 1 1/2 cups pecan halves
- 1/2 cup semi-sweet chocolate chips

Instructions:

1. **Prepare the filling**:
   Preheat the oven to 350°F (175°C). In a large bowl, whisk together corn syrup, brown sugar, eggs, melted butter, vanilla extract, and salt. Stir in pecans and chocolate chips.
2. **Assemble the pie**:
   Pour the filling into the prepared pie crust, spreading it evenly.
3. **Bake**:
   Bake for 45-50 minutes, or until the pie is set and the filling has thickened. Let the pie cool completely before slicing and serving.

Chocolate Chip Banana Muffins

Ingredients:

- 1 1/2 cups all-purpose flour
- 1/2 tsp baking soda
- 1/4 tsp salt
- 1/2 cup sugar
- 2 large ripe bananas, mashed
- 1/2 cup unsalted butter, melted
- 1 tsp vanilla extract
- 1 large egg
- 1/2 cup semi-sweet chocolate chips

Instructions:

1. **Prepare the batter**:
   Preheat the oven to 350°F (175°C). Grease or line a muffin tin with paper liners. In a bowl, whisk together flour, baking soda, salt, and sugar. In another bowl, combine mashed bananas, melted butter, vanilla extract, and egg. Add the wet ingredients to the dry ingredients and stir until just combined. Fold in chocolate chips.
2. **Bake the muffins**:
   Divide the batter evenly among the muffin cups. Bake for 18-20 minutes, or until a toothpick inserted comes out clean. Let the muffins cool before serving.

Chocolate Zucchini Cake

Ingredients:

- 2 cups all-purpose flour
- 1/2 cup unsweetened cocoa powder
- 1 1/2 tsp baking powder
- 1/2 tsp baking soda
- 1/2 tsp salt
- 1 tsp cinnamon
- 1/2 cup vegetable oil
- 1 1/4 cups sugar
- 2 large eggs
- 1 tsp vanilla extract
- 1 1/2 cups grated zucchini (about 2 medium zucchini)
- 1/2 cup semi-sweet chocolate chips

Instructions:

1. **Prepare the batter**:
   Preheat the oven to 350°F (175°C). Grease and flour an 8x8-inch baking pan. In a large bowl, whisk together flour, cocoa powder, baking powder, baking soda, salt, and cinnamon. In another bowl, whisk together oil, sugar, eggs, and vanilla extract. Stir in the grated zucchini. Gradually add the dry ingredients to the wet ingredients and stir until combined. Fold in chocolate chips.
2. **Bake the cake**:
   Pour the batter into the prepared pan and bake for 30-35 minutes, or until a toothpick inserted into the center comes out clean. Let cool before slicing and serving.

Chocolate Cherry Clafoutis

Ingredients:

- 1 1/2 cups fresh cherries, pitted
- 1/2 cup whole milk
- 1/2 cup heavy cream
- 3 large eggs
- 1/2 cup sugar
- 1 tsp vanilla extract
- 1/4 tsp salt
- 1/2 cup all-purpose flour
- Powdered sugar, for dusting

Instructions:

1. **Prepare the clafoutis**:
   Preheat the oven to 350°F (175°C). Butter a 9-inch pie dish or similar baking dish. Spread the cherries evenly in the bottom of the dish.
2. **Make the batter**:
   In a blender or mixing bowl, combine milk, heavy cream, eggs, sugar, vanilla extract, salt, and flour. Blend or whisk until smooth. Pour the batter over the cherries.
3. **Bake the clafoutis**:
   Bake for 35-40 minutes, or until the clafoutis is puffed and golden. Let it cool slightly, then dust with powdered sugar before serving.

Chocolate Chip Blondies

Ingredients:

- 2 cups all-purpose flour
- 1 tsp baking powder
- 1/2 tsp salt
- 1 cup unsalted butter, softened
- 1 cup brown sugar, packed
- 1 large egg
- 1 tsp vanilla extract
- 1 1/2 cups semi-sweet chocolate chips

Instructions:

1. **Prepare the batter**:
   Preheat the oven to 350°F (175°C) and line an 8x8-inch baking pan with parchment paper. In a bowl, whisk together flour, baking powder, and salt. In a separate bowl, cream butter and brown sugar until light and fluffy. Add the egg and vanilla extract, and mix well. Gradually add the dry ingredients and stir until just combined. Fold in chocolate chips.
2. **Bake the blondies**:
   Spread the batter evenly in the prepared pan. Bake for 25-30 minutes, or until a toothpick inserted comes out clean. Let cool before slicing into squares.

Chocolate Churros

Ingredients:

- 1 cup water
- 1/2 cup unsalted butter
- 1 tbsp sugar
- 1/4 tsp salt
- 1 cup all-purpose flour
- 2 large eggs
- 1/2 cup semi-sweet chocolate chips
- 1/2 cup sugar (for coating)
- 1 tsp ground cinnamon (for coating)
- Vegetable oil for frying

Instructions:

1. **Prepare the churro dough:**
   In a saucepan, bring water, butter, sugar, and salt to a boil. Remove from heat and stir in flour until the mixture comes together in a dough. Let the dough cool for a few minutes, then add eggs one at a time, mixing well between each addition.
2. **Make the chocolate filling:**
   In a microwave-safe bowl, melt chocolate chips until smooth. Set aside to cool slightly.
3. **Fry the churros:**
   Heat oil in a deep frying pan over medium-high heat. Spoon the churro dough into a piping bag with a star tip. Pipe the dough into the hot oil in 4-6 inch strips. Fry until golden brown, about 2-3 minutes per side. Remove the churros from the oil and drain on paper towels.
4. **Coat the churros:**
   In a small bowl, combine sugar and cinnamon. While still warm, roll the churros in the cinnamon-sugar mixture. Drizzle with melted chocolate before serving.

www.ingramcontent.com/pod-product-compliance
Lightning Source LLC
LaVergne TN
LVHW081335060526
838201LV00055B/2655